ORANGE COUNTY SCHOOL BOARD
PURCHASED WITH
ECIA CHAPTER 11 FUNDS
068-C2 — 93-94

David Robinson

PHOTO CREDITS
The National Basketball Association
Allsport: cover, pg. 25 and 30
Andrew Bernstein: pg. 2 & 3, 9, 10, 14, 17, 21, 22
Nathaniel Butler: pg. 6, 18, 26, 29
Jon SooHoo: pg. 13

Text copyright © 1991 by The Child's World, Inc.
All rights reserved. No part of this book may be
reproduced or utilized in any form or by any means
without written permission from the Publisher.
Printed in the United States of America.

Distributed to Schools and Libraries
in Canada by
SAUNDERS BOOK COMPANY
Box 308
Collingwood, Ontario, Canada 69Y3Z7 / (800) 461-9120

Library of Congress Cataloging-in-Publication Data
Rothaus, James.
David Robinson / Jim Rothaus.
p. cm.
Summary: A sports profile of the San Antonio Spurs' David Robinson.
ISBN 0-89565-784-8
1. Robinson, David, 1965-   —Juvenile literature.
2. Basketball players–United States–Biography–Juvenile literature.
3. San Antonio Spurs (Basketball team)–Juvenile literature.
[1. Robinson, David, 1965-   2. Basketball players.
3. Afro-Americans–Biography.] I. Title.
GV884.R615R68 1991   91-24880
796.323′092–dc20   CIP
[B]   AC

David Robinson

by James R. Rothaus

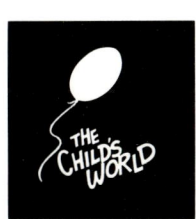

David Robinson in a Spurs' uniform.

Two Years of Waiting

On July 25, 1989, basketball fans in San Antonio got their first look at their new star. After two years of waiting, they were finally going to see David Robinson in a Spurs' uniform. San Antonio had taken Robinson with the first pick in the 1987 National Basketball Association draft. Everybody knew Robinson was the best player in that draft. But he wouldn't be able to play right away. He had to finish his tour of duty in the Naval Reserve.

Had to Serve His Country

Robinson went to college at the U.S. Naval Academy. This meant that when his college days were over, Robinson had to serve his country, perhaps for as long as five years. When Robinson graduated, the U.S. Navy agreed to let Robinson go two years after he finished college. Then he would be able to play professional basketball. The Spurs drafted Robinson in 1987, knowing that he couldn't play until the 1989-90 season. They were willing to wait because Robinson was worth waiting for.

Robinson was worth waiting for.

David shines on both offense and defense.

NCAA Tournament Upset

During his last two years at Navy, the 7-foot 1-inch Robinson stood tall over the rest of college basketball. He scored a ton of points, grabbed rebounds in bunches, and blocked shots right and left. As a junior at Navy, Robinson led his team to the NCAA tournament. The Midshipmen shocked everyone by beating powerful Syracuse in the tournament. Even more amazing was that the game was played on Syracuse's home court. But the large crowd couldn't help Syracuse.

College Player of the Year

The Orangemen couldn't stop Robinson from scoring. And they had no one to match him in the middle. The Navy center grabbed all the big rebounds and blocked a lot of Syracuse shots. The whole nation now knew about David Robinson. The next year, the Navy center led his team to the NCAA tournament again. The Midshipmen lost to Michigan in the first round. But Robinson was named the college player of the year. He was also picked as a first-team All-American at center.

Robinson named All-American.

Robinson plays on Olympic Team.

Lieutenant Junior Grade

Robinson graduated from Navy, but his tour of duty lasted two more years. He rose to the rank of lieutenant junior grade. He also played basketball on Navy all-star teams. In 1988 he was picked for the U.S. basketball team in the Summer Olympics in Seoul, South Korea. Robinson was expected to be the star on this team. He was expected to lead the United States to the gold medal. Robinson didn't play badly, but he wasn't a star, either. The United States wound up third and took the bronze medal.

Spurs Need a Lot of Help

After the Olympics, Robinson went back to his service in the Naval Reserve. San Antonio would have to wait one more year to have Robinson in the lineup. His Navy duty ended in the summer of 1989. Robinson then reported to the Spurs, who really needed all the help they could get. In the last two seasons, San Antonio had a record of 52-112. The Spurs were one of the worst teams in the NBA. But now they had David Robinson. His first game with the team was on July 25, 1989. It was an intersquad game.

A defensive standout.

Robinson makes the difference.

Robinson Stars Right Away

Robinson showed right away he was the best player on the squad. In front of a large crowd, Robinson gave the cheering fans their money's worth. He scored thirty-one points, grabbed seventeen rebounds, and blocked ten shots. Four months later, the Spurs opened the season at home against the powerful Los Angeles Lakers. Robinson scored twenty-three points and had seventeen rebounds. San Antonio won 106-98. Robinson had only one blocked shot, but it was a big one.

No Magic For Los Angeles

With San Antonio leading 72-70 in the third quarter, Laker guard Magic Johnson drove to the basket. Robinson went up and blocked Magic's layup. San Antonio got the ball, went down the court, and scored. The Spurs held the lead the rest of the way. "My job," Robinson said after the game, "is to keep opponents from taking the ball to the hoop." When Magic tried to go to the basket, Robinson did his job. In the Laker locker room, a newspaper reporter asked Johnson about Robinson.

David jams up the middle.

He has the talent to do it all.

This Guy Is a Rookie?

"Some rookies are never really rookies. Robinson's one of them," Magic said. The San Antonio center never did play like a rookie. He was a star from the very beginning. "If he's still learning the game, I'd hate to see him when he knows it cold," said New Jersey guard Mookie Blaylock. "He has the talent all us big guys only hope and dream for," said San Antonio center Caldwell Jones. Jones should know about great centers. He had been a professional basketball player for seventeen years.

Surprise Team in the League

Jones had played against all the best centers. Kareem Abdul-Jabbar. Bill Walton. Moses Malone. Robert Parish. Hakeem Olajuwon. Patrick Ewing. Jones was glad David Robinson was a teammate, not an opponent. "No other big guy I've ever seen is anywhere as quick and fast as him," Jones said of Robinson. "That's what sets David apart." The Spurs and Robinson became the surprise team in the league. In 1989 San Antonio finished second to last in the NBA's Midwest Division. In 1990 the Spurs took first place.

A quick and fast big man.

From losers to winners.

NBA Rookie of the Year

David Robinson was a big reason the Spurs went from losers to winners so fast. He finished the season with a scoring average of 24.3 points per game, tenth best in the NBA. He also pulled down 12 rebounds a game, second only to Houston's Hakeem Olajuwon. Robinson also averaged 3.8 blocked shots. Only Olajuwon and Patrick Ewing of New York slapped away more shots. Robinson was named the NBA's Rookie of the Year. He was also picked to the second team of the league's All-Defensive squad.

Attention Is Embarrassing

San Antonio ended the season with a 56-26 record. The Spurs beat Denver in the first round of the playoffs, but then lost to Portland in the second round. Despite the defeat, it was a super year for the team. Much of the credit for San Antonio's success was given to Robinson. "All the attention I've received is embarrassing," Robinson said. "I'm still trying to make my place in the league. . . . It's easy to lose your identity, particularly when you don't even <u>have</u> an identity."

The Spurs are on the move.

With Robinson aboard the Spurs can win it all.

The Team of the 1990s?

But Robinson does have an identity. He is the best player on what may soon be the best team in the NBA. Robinson isn't San Antonio's only good young player. The Spurs also have future stars in forward Sean Elliott, and guards Willie Anderson and Rod Strickland. Experts are calling San Antonio the team of the 1990s. Fans in San Antonio are expecting the Spurs to bring home several NBA titles. If the team does, David Robinson will be a major reason.